All Scripture references taken from the KJV of the HOLY Bible, unless otherwise indicated.

Players Gonna Play: Don't Let Player Drama and Dating Trauma Steal Your Future

by Dr. Marlene Miles

Freshwater Press, USA

ISBN: 978-1-960150-89-9

Paperback Version

Copyright 2023 by Dr. Marlene Miles

All rights reserved. No portion of this book may be copied, photocopied, emailed or held in any type of retrieval system without the express written approval of the Author.

Table of Contents

The Dating Game 6
What Did I Just Agree To? 14
Players Gonna Play 21
Mommy, Dear 29
Player, Player 34
Daddy's Boy 38
Where Do We Go From Here? 40
I HATE Spirit Spouse 42
Sinvitations 50
Polygamous People 53
He's My Covering, *Right*? 64
License to Thrill 67
Bed Defilement 70
Married to the Mob 74
Make It Stop! 82
Let's Get Healed of Traumas 88
Prayer Resources 94
Dear Reader: 95
Other books by this author 96

Player

A player is usually a boy who makes you feel special. He makes you feel like you are the only girl in his life, when really you are just one in 100.

They flirt with other people, not just you. They talk to you all day, then the next day they ignore you. They send you mixed messages, and you're not sure whether he likes you or not.

You can't keep your mind off him, even though you know you're nothing to him.

Urban Dictionary

https://www.urbandictionary.com/define.php?term=Player

Players Gonna Play

Don't Let Player Drama and Dating Trauma Steal Your Future

Holy Spirit, teach.

Amen.

The Dating Game

We should not live our lives in fear, but there are potential traumas all around us. It's why the Bible says to walk circumspectly which means carefully, considering all possible circumstances and consequences. That is very similar to saying, *head on swivel,* but it is far more than that. It is more than just what you see. All our choices should be made using the most knowledge and Wisdom, with careful consideration of every possible outcome. Just living for right now, or for today is not all there is. Thinking like that can land anyone of us in a world of trouble.

See then that ye walk circumspectly, not as fools, but as wise, Redeeming the time, because the days are evil. Ephesians 5:15-16

Even dating can be confusing, and have trauma attached to it. No wonder so many cultures arrange marriages for their children; it can be treacherous out there. In societies where the parents do not choose their children's spouses, because of potential or previous dating trauma, some people no longer date, staying away from it altogether. Some do date on a limited basis.

Others dive in with reckless abandon; it is what they do, maybe *only* what they do giving no thought to consequences, or only physical consequences. There are serial daters, rolling stones, old gangsters (OG's), and *players* who are seeking the good life. That good life usually revolves around partying, drinking, using recreational drugs, and looking for frequent, or *free* sex. All of which can lead to serious natural and spiritual problems.

Dinah

In the Bible, one day Jacob's daughter, Dinah went out by herself and was abducted and raped, (Genesis 34:5, 13, 27). The child of a prince with 10 or 11 brothers and no doubt, servants of many varieties didn't need to go anywhere by herself, for any reason. Royalty and children with well-off parents can sometimes be rebellious and often want to get out of the house. As is human nature, the reason Dinah may not have wanted anyone to go with her is that she was going out to do something she should not have been doing.

    She didn't go out to meet a guy, or for a date, but she did get seen by a fellow who grabbed her and raped her, Dinah was abducted and raped near the city of Shechem, by Shechem, son of Hamor the Hivite, (Genesis 30). People, especially women of high estate did not usually go places alone, unescorted. For this reason, this fellow may have thought she was a commoner, and up for grabs--, plus in my opinion, he was a thuggish brut. This abduction and rape set up a whole cascade of horrible events.

There is treachery out there. You have to be wise, be prepared, and have discernment in life, wherever you go and in whatever you do. Don't rebel against parents, leadership, or authority, and *head on swivel*, and mind on God.

Now Dinah, the daughter Leah had borne to Jacob, went out to visit the women of the land, (Genesis 34:1 NIV)

No, Dinah did not go out for brunch or coffee – the girls/women of the land are the *idols* of that country. Did she not want anyone to know what she was doing? The Bible doesn't say, but we do know that she was alone.

Just as the lone gazelle gets attacked by a lion, opportunists, such as *players* look for susceptible females who are often alone and find them to be easier prey.

Don't be prey.

Delilah

Delilah was a seductress. She was on assignment to take Samson down, and she did. Delilah personifies the *spirit of lust*. (Judges 6:4). L*ust* is what drives many to "date" because lusting people are looking for people to score with. In the case of Samson, it made him putty in Delilah's hands.

In societies immemorial, men are encouraged to do what they want, sow wild oats, and conquer women. Women are told to do none of that. I'm still trying to reconcile in my mind, where the women are that the men are supposed to be sowing wild oats *with* supposed to come from? By the same token there have been seductresses through the ages, femme fatales and agents who use sex against their targets. All of these are as dangerous as Delilah was to Samson.

David

While the men were supposed to be out at war, David was home walking on the roof of his palace. As he looked, he saw a woman bathing, "and the woman was very beautiful" (2 Samuel 11:2). He asked about her and found she was Bathsheba, the wife of Uriah the Hittite

David lusted for Bathsheba, beautiful or not, he was watching her bathe, that's like looking at pornography. In that instance, *lust* would be sparked in him. If he didn't have it before, it was the right time for lust to jump into him. *Lust* is a player *spirit* and when David joined forces with it, it made David a player. Yes, King David, a player.

I ask this question of Bathsheba who was no Delilah, what are you supposed to do when the **King** sends for you? In the book of Eshter, Vashti didn't appear for King Ahasuerus, and she was put away. Esther did, and she was promoted.

What are you supposed to do when you are already married to someone else? When a person of high authority *sends* for you, you must answer, or face consequences, I'm sure.

This wasn't really dating but you see how dangerous this was--, and still. You can see how dangerous it is *"out there."*

Solomon

Solomon had 700 wives and 300 concubines, and still ended up in idolatry. Hard to believe that Solomon had **time** to worship anything or anyone with all those women to either tend to, or to amuse him. Of course, if he worshipped the women, he indirectly worshipped whatever deities they worshipped. That is built in to idolatry.

God told him not to marry all those pagan women, but he did it anyway--, because of *lust*. Solomon started out so well, but was a chip off the old David and off the old Bathsheba block.

OG's (old gangsters) who are skirt chasers are so proud to transfer their prized womanizing *spirit* and behavior to their sons. It's why many of them want sons, and they think this is what makes a male a man. David transferred this *spirit* to Solomon? Most likely. After all it is in Solomon's blood to chase women.

Of course, *lust* is a *spirit*. A person can lust for all kinds of things--, food, money, not just sex. People usually don't *date* for food, but I don't put that past anyone these days. so, this book will focus on the strong desire for sex between two people.

What Did I Just Agree To?

Ladies, when you sleep with a person you may be thinking you're giving **temporary access to your body**, but it is much more than that.

They call it consent; they call it consensual, but how can you give consent to something that you don't know anything about? If you don't even know what you gave consent to. Agreeing to sex, there is so much fine print that is so fine that you can't even see it.

Sex cuts covenant. Sex involves blood; it forms covenant. If it is not a Godly covenant, then it is the facsimile of it, it forms a soul tie with the devil right in the middle of it.

Yes, every sex act is either OF GOD, sanctioned by God, or not. Every time.

By having sex with a person, you are saying, *Here's my soul–, take it.* You give full access to it. You give access to your mind, will, intellect and emotions. By exchanging your soul for sex – usually illicit sex, you are putting at risk, or giving up some, most, or all of the virtues and blessings that your soul possesses. It's complicated, but it is true.

Entering into that act, what either person thinks is happening is happening in the physical, but so much more than that is happening. While men very often think they are forming a situationship and women probably think *relationship,* much more than that occurs. The sex act gets in your head, into your soul and in your spirit. It forms a covenant/soul tie, whether you intend for it to or not. That is, <u>if you're human.</u>

Transactional beings don't work that way, that's another whole thing. There are those who can say it didn't mean anything--, **_we should question their humanity._** But spiritually everything that happens because of sex happens no matter what each or either party involved *decides* or agrees that it *means*.

Doing this act gets into you – literally. And this is especially true since women mostly take on the nature of the man after the consummation. But the Bible says the two become one, so seems to me each can take on the other's nature.

> What? Know ye not that he which is joined to an harlot is one body? For two, saith he, shall become one flesh. But he that is joined unto the Lord is one spirit. 1 Corinthians 6:16-17

Whomever you hook up with you join with their human spirit, **and** whatever other *spirits* are in them. The Holy Spirit of God is the only one that openly and honestly asks for permission and invitation. The rest of them Bogard their way into the lives of anyone that they can. By consenting, you didn't just give **temporary** access to your body to this guy. The access that you've allowed goes far past your body, and timewise, far past the sex act itself. If this were a concert, this guy has been given full access and has a backstage pass; he can go anywhere as it pertains to you. You can do the same regarding him, but did you know this?

As a matter of fact, you're married to him; you've made *covenant* with him. *Goes-in-to* equals **married**; that is, married to whatever *spirit* or *spirits* that are in him (his demons) now.

Getting out of this is going to take *waaaay* more work than getting into it, that is, if you want to get out of it. That also depends on if the other party wants to get out of it, too. Soul ties can be maintained for decades. Someone could be soul tied to you and you've forgotten all about them, and vice versa. A person could be soul tied to anything, a place, a time, a food, a song.

Being in deep and unable to get out could be why they say people *fall* in love – well, into *lust*. People can fall into a whole mess.

Flee sexual immorality. Every sin that a man does is outside the body, but he who commits sexual immorality sins against his own body, (1 Corinthians 6:18).

So, when that bad boy turns on you, and he will turn on you, he may be saying to you in a heated argument, *"Wow, you were never like this before, you've changed."*

You proudly say as you're giving it back to him as good as he is giving it to you, *"All this bad stuff—I learned it from you."* And you're so proud to say it. Really, he just pulled you down into the flesh, so now both of you are in the flesh. If he is just a flesh creature, he was already in the flesh and if you are supposedly saved, instead of you pulling him up, he pulled you down.

God can't do anything for either of you if you're both in the flesh.

The person with the stronger spirit will win the other one to his or her way of thinking and being. God is the strongest, but the person who is practicing, worshipping and serving whatever *god* they are serving with the most dedication has the stronger, most insistent spirit.

So, you may have learned to be evil from this undercover evil guy. Is that what you wanted to learn, how to fight dirty, how to be petty, and how to go tit-for-tat?

While you were wasting time on this wrong guy for you, you may not have ever been in the right place to even meet the right person that God has for you. That could have been that man's whole assignment against you; be a BLOCKER. His assignment could have been something like: Keep her from her destiny meetings and connections.

When we are saved, we are supposed to be married to Christ, if we are saved, we should be taking on the nature of Christ, not the nature of a player and his or her demons.

Players Gonna Play

You players out there, player is a *spirit* and it is demonic. It is not from God or of God, sanctioned by God, approved by God or **blessed** by God; it is demonic.

Player is a *spirit of lust*. Delilah *spirit* is the *player spirit.* Bad as it was, at least Delilah knew she was on assignment, whereas, some of these who are for the streets don't even know that they are working for the devil to ruin the lives of the people they meet--, and *date*.

Players think they are *all that,* and they really think they are bringing pleasure. but at what cost? THERE IS A COST. There is no free lunch. **There is no free sex.** The <u>cost</u> is in the fine print, and the fine-fine print. That illegible and invisible *print* outlines the covenant that is made when you have sex, even one time, with another. Body parts are not ala carte and separated from the rest of your body and your entire being.

Ladies, don't smile, women can have this *spirit* too, IN SPADES. In today's society women think that they can give it as good as men. A woman can have this *spirit* on her own accord. Where'd she get it? It could have transferred to her from a sex partner; evil *spirits* are transferred easily through sex. It could be where she got it.

Any human can pick up an evil *spirit* from what they look at, participate in, and think about. The default in the Earth is the devil's kingdom. We are in it, not supposed to be *of* it, but we are saturated in it. The Holy Spirit has to ask because His realm is the third Heaven and we are in the first Heaven, here on Earth.

If you are saved, women especially, you **say** you're saved, or believe you're saved, you don't do any of this stuff. None of it.

I know avid church goers—some who hold ***positions*** in their church-- who believe having a boyfriend, shacking up is fine as long as they go to church on Sunday, as if that will redeem them for six days of sin. It is not and does not.

These people either don't have the Holy Spirit, or have turned off the HOLY SPIRIT **Notifications** in their spirit. They are ignoring Him and are thereby grieving or quenching the HOLY SPIRIT. That happens when they are paying attention to the leadings and promptings of the Holy Spirit as He tries to convict of sin and get them back on the right path for their life again. That's where the blessings are, the successes, joy, and peace, in the Holy Spirit.

Living as a sinner while serving in the church is not okay. *When* the rules got relaxed, where you can be unmarried and have a boyfriend, but we accepted in the church, or church leadership, as if you are legally married to that person -- I'm not sure. But we all know that just because everyone else is doing it, does not make it okay. It makes it popular and accepted by sinners, but not by God.

First of all, whether he goes to church or not, once you declare yourself a church person, saying that you're a good girl, and you never do this; you've *never* even done this before, yet you sleep with this new guy in your life, anyway--, you are now a **joke**. To that man, you are just like the rest of *them*--, just like the women who do not even say they are saved.

And, to him, you are just like all those folks in the Church that he believes are hypocrites. This is his main excuse for not going to church in the first place. AND, after this, he may not ever want to get saved---

Well, unless he has some kind of life crisis and needs to call on God.

Still some who have a crisis and call on God, then once their crisis is over -- they go right back to what they were doing before the crisis. No, they don't think anything is wrong with that, because that's what everyone else is doing. Sadly, humankind is just like this, all through the Bible and also these days.

Don't push it; God says He will not always strive with man.

They just live their lives as they choose, until there is a crisis. Once the crisis comes, you whip out your *God card* as if God is an insurance plan for when you need Him. When the crisis is over, and you're fine again, you put that card back in your wallet, and save it for another day.

But that is not how God works. God is a God of relationship, not just transactions.

Why might they think such a thing? Players do not understand relationships. It's very telling in how they treat people. To them, dates are for when they need something, or want something. After they get that *something*, you may not see or hear from them again, or until they have that *need* again.

You may ask them, *what is a relationship?* They have no idea. And *how do you conduct a relationship*? They do not know.

RUN!

Players are on a demonic assignment, but often don't even realize it. What is the assignment? The devil is running this, so here's the end game. They are assigned to:

- Wreck a life.
- Jack a life.
- Mark territory.
- Ruin her destiny.
- Keep her from marrying anyone else.
- Stagnate a destiny.
- STOP a destiny.
- Steal virtue.

- Cover or steal glory.
- Cover or steal her star.
- Steal money.
- Keep her in poverty.
- Lock her down.
- Give her kids that she will have to take care of.
- Waste a beautiful girl's youth, then drop her at a certain age and get someone younger. He is looking for fresh supply all the time.

I have just described the behavior and objectives of a *spirit spouse*. If this is a real person versus a *spirit*, this person, on assignment has become *as* a **physical spirit spouse**. Encountering or getting involved with this type of person could make her whole life and that of her kids trauma-filled, relegating them to survival mode, for a season, or even all of their lives.

The player's assignment is to traumatize their victim, whether they realize they are doing it or not. The assignment is from hell, and the devil loves trauma and uses trauma.

Once traumatized – the devil can get in there, especially if she defaults to Survival Mode which is a flesh mode, and stays there, lives there, all of her life. If a person is in flesh mode, how will they live by faith, and please God?

But without faith it is impossible to please him: for he that cometh to **God** must believe that he is, and that he is a rewarder of them that diligently seek him. (Hebrews 11:6)

Mommy, Dear

Some of you may look at your mom and ask, *Why is mom so stressed?* She's hyper all the time. She needs to chill and relax.

She can't: she's in Survival Mode, baby. She's got two or three kids, raising them by herself. She's got one job, or two, or three. If she has one job, that may not be enough. If she's got two jobs, she's tired. If she has three jobs, she is exhausted. She's in survival mode trying to take care of her kids, so what happened to her, doesn't happen to them.

That was financial survival mode. Have you ever considered she could be in an emotional survival mode, as well? Where and who is her emotional support--, especially while she's trying to be emotionally supportive to all of you?

This is a spiritual problem as much as it is a natural problem, so mom really needs to be praying and breaking strongholds, yokes, bondages, and healing her foundation.

But in the natural, some stuff she did in her 20's is still beating up on her life right now, and she's 40. Some of the problems are you, for one. For two, three, and four: your brother and sister, and that man that keeps coming in and out of her life.

That man--, he's back again. She's hoping that maybe this time he's serious. Maybe this time he's changed. Maybe this time he will stay. And, if he stays, maybe he will help. Just because a man is *there* doesn't mean that he plans to support the household or the family at all. Some players choose a successful woman so that if he ever has a need, he can come to her house and live there, or at least get a good meal and stay a few nights.

He's at least oppressed by the devil; he's demonized, only a demonized male would think like this. But he might know how to *play* nice, act nice, act polished, but really, he's not any of that – it's all about him.

There is another variation of this, the man that won't leave a woman alone. He is a stalker or human persecutor. That individual is also demonically charged. Don't play with it; pray against it. There's a prayer for that, and it is very effective!

https://bridemovement.com/ultimate-freedom-from-human-persecutors/

Dangerous and judgmental prayers are for Protestant Christians in right standing with God. Be sure that is you, so you don't make matters worse by praying unauthorized prayers.

It's 20 years later, she's still trying to fix what she did in her 20's, whether she was deceived, tricked, and traumatized by a boy, or whether she was rebellious and participated on her own accord.

It's 30 years later, she's *still* paying for it… still trying to sort it out; even her kids are trying to help her out of her plight. Will she be 60 years old and still trying to fix this? What is *this*? The *this* is what she consented to when she consented to the first player to come into her life, or the next one, or the next one.

Could it be that she is paying for not only the sins of her youth, but also the sins of her ancestors and doesn't even know it?

WILL YOURS? Will your children and future generations have to pay for the mistakes of your youth, or your ancestral iniquity? If you aren't aware that you have any of that, and haven't done anything about it, they will.

And thou take of their daughters unto thy sons, and their daughters go a whoring after their gods, and make thy sons go a whoring after their gods, (Genesis 34:16-19

Your kids will also be paying if you do not deal spiritually with your foundation and the reasons why you are as you are, the reasons why your family is as it is, and the reasons why things happen to you and your family as they do.

Flee also youthful lusts but follow righteousness, faith, charity, peace with them that call on the Lord out of a pure heart. 2 Timothy 2:22

Player, Player

Here, I expound on a story that I first shared in my book, **The Devil Loves Trauma.** It is a true story, but I will use no names.

    I know a man who is obsessed with sex, there are a lot of them out there. I've met more than one. Out of his own mouth he stated that he would like to be like a rooster in a hen house and just do that all day long. This man **believes he's saved**, he believes he is going to Heaven, but this is how he conducts his daily life. The *spirit* that spoke that, through him---, the *spirit* that lives in him is *lust*. *That spirit* wants this man and any man that it influences or inhabits to fulfill *lust*. But lust cannot be fulfilled, or satiated. It can be temporarily satisfied--, for a day, or an hour or two, but then it will want something else. Lust *wants* all day long.

The Lord is my shepherd; I shall not want. Psalm 23:1

By restoring a man's soul, God gives deliverance to a person. If *want* is taken away from a man that means that greed, lust and dissatisfaction are no longer in a person's soul. God and a relationship with God is very satisfying.

Seek that.

If hen house man's real human spirit doesn't object to the rooster in the hen house plan and this man gets delivered of that plan, then this *spirit,* will have its way by the man having what the man is saying. It won't be pleasant, no matter what he thinks. It will be bondage. It will be hell.

I was told a story years ago of an enlisted man in the military who wouldn't or couldn't stop smoking. His Sergeant made him put a bucket over his head and chain smoke one cigarette after the other.

The man became ill of all the smoke and disgusted of smoking. He quit smoking as soon as he finished that pack, and the bucket was removed from his head. I'm sure it was horrible. Being **made** to do something to excess, *ad nauseum*, over and again with no break certainly takes the pleasure out of the activity.

Rooster in a hen house? Being MADE to do it? It will not be pleasant.

But if this man does not take back, rescind his words, renounce them --, he may have what he says. No, I don't mean he will turn into a rooster, but he will be forced 24/7 to perform rooster duties. How so? Sex addicts cannot get satisfaction. Sex fiends, nymphomaniacs are driven by the *spirit* that is in them to constantly have sex.

In this way, the man is agreeing with Hell via the *spirit* that is in him, having all the "fun." And have all the bragging rights with his friends. Of course, the enticement is that this is fun, this will be fun, this is cool, this will make you manly, this will make you look good to your bruh's.

Again, unless you know all the fine print of what you are consenting to, do not consent to anything. The enticement is always good, but the reality can be brutal bondage.

Daddy's Boy

Roostering in a henhouse? Where would he get such an idea? Is this the directive of this man's natural daddy? Did his daddy put this idea in his mind since he was a young boy? Whether or not he remembers his father saying that to him, or his grandfather, or his uncle said it, it's in there. It's really in the blood already; it is an ancestral assignment; this man is just walking it out. Further, Henhouse Man has one or more natural sons, and he has taught them the exact same thing.

Now is it an ancestral assignment because this is the idol that the family worships? Scoring against women? Or, does this family owe for some ancient favor and this is how the idol collects worship? Is this a joke, where an elder of the family spoke this to the kid, just to see what the kid would do, and he internalized it? All of us can think of the kid that gets tossed in the lake to see if he can swim, even though he's had no lessons. Was this a gag, and the kid fell for it and took it as the blueprint of his life?

Is this already an assignment of the enemy where the male made a covenant, knowingly, or unknowingly, and now he can't satisfy this *lust* demon? Did he pray for sex, and sex, and more sex as a teenager, and now that is what he is assigned to do?

Or, was some trauma imposed on the male and this is the demon that rushed in? And then he accepted it because at first, like that one cigarette, he felt so good. So he kept inviting it, and doing it and seeking it, and doing it again until *lust* made a home in that gentleman?

Where Do We Go From Here?

In Eternity, that *spirit—invited or not,* is not getting into Heaven. So where will this "saved" man be? Where will this man's soul go after death? There is no afterparty, after death, People. Where is his soul going if it can't get into Heaven and if this *spirit* has joined with his spirit, it has married him? Where will he be?

We need to let the Holy Spirit send us notifications. We need to turn **Notifications** back on from the Holy Spirit. We don't quench the Spirit that is trying to save our lives – our Earth lives, and also our Eternal lives. The Holy Spirit is trying to help us reach our Godly eternal destination. When the Holy Spirit gives you pause, stop, listen and obey. When the

Holy Spirit says don't do a thing, don't do that thing. When the Holy Spirit says, No, the answer is, No! When the Holy Spirit says, Run!

RUN!

Folks can be harassed by the devil, oppressed by the devil, or possessed by the devil, or any of his *spirits*. Those who are possessed, owned, and captive do what the devil wants them to do; they have no choice. They can fight it here on Earth, but after Earth, there is nothing they can do, but suffer, eternally. There is no afterparty. There is no do over after death.

Before you leave this planet, before you go from here, get everything, I mean everything out of you that is not from God or of God. Everything in you that doesn't, can't, and won't worship God has to get out of you, so your final destination from here will be with God, and not in hell, in perpetual bondage and torment.

I HATE Spirit Spouse

Dating trauma is real to the victim **and** to the oppressive person causing the trauma. You may be wondering why I am calling dating trauma. As stated, there is spiritual trauma, there is soul trauma. No bones need to be broken for a person to sustain a trauma or an injury. Soft tissue injuries are very real and painful physically. Spiritual trauma can be even more devastating in the spirit. We attend quickly to physical trauma in our daily lives, but sometimes spiritual trauma is under the radar. Sometimes spiritual trauma is not even detected until weeks, months, or years later. So, spiritual traumas that open spiritual doors linger; so much is happening behind the scenes and unless we are spiritually aware, or connected with others who are spiritually aware and will tell us what is going on, we may be clueless.

It seems this man who wants to be like a rooster is applying for the job of *spirit spouse* and training his kids in the same way. In this way, his children will pay for his sins, and/or the iniquity of sins in their bloodline. He or someone in their bloodline signed all the males in that family up for this bondage. I cannot say more right now. *I can't* because I hate *spirit spouse* with *perfect hate.*

Spirit spouse's job is serial defilement, among other things defilement of a human being is trauma. Defilements come right at the edge of breakthrough. Something good is just about to happen in your life, and you get defiled. Poof! It's gone. This is one of the ways the devil stops your breakthroughs, steals or stops your promotions and successes, and put you on an evil timeline, or a satanic calendar or satanic clock.

Any man who desires and is involved in stud service relationships and situationships, in the Earth, while he is at least physically living this life, is auditioning for the job of *spirit spouse*. He is technically a *physical spirit spouse*—a player, blocking good things in your life. Blocking marriage. Blocking natural children, or giving you so many children, and usually at a very young age, that it frustrates and traumatizes you. *Spirit spouse* steals virtues, wastes time, takes glory. OG's often present as *physical spirit spouses*, and we all need deliverance if we are victims to any of this.

Of course, they have evil fallen angels for that, but this human male may already be a *physical spirit spouse* to any number of women, or men. Spirit spouse in the spirit is gender fluid; it changes into whatever it needs to in order to attack its victims. It is a dangerous, stubborn *spirit*. Don't invite it in any way. Fast and pray and seek deliverance if you have one (or more).

Stud service men really think they are so desirable, but they do not realize the **TRAUMA** they inflict on women, and eventually the children they have. They are working like the devil, *for* the devil. The reward is usually sex and bragging rights, to your friends or for your ego, and that by deception.

Another notch on your belt...

Pride is another one of those evil *spirits* traveling with *lust*.

Pray God that whatever you are doing, whatever you think is fun, or living is not traumatizing the people you know and encounter, else, you are on **remote** for the devil without even realizing it.

How so, you wonder. You left her broken hearted, with or without kids, she may be soul tied, possibly. She's wondering if you're coming back, are you ever coming back? Maybe she is believing that you will if you're a really good liar.

She's wondering when you don't come back, or take her texts or call her back--what's wrong with her? Why DID YOU LEAVE? That man told you that you were the one, wifey material.

Of course, he did; he wanted to get the most out of you as possible.

As soon as he said that to you, I bet you started cooking for him, and doing all kinds of domestic things for him. I bet he ate good when he came to your house. Your Netflix and chill is legendary, isn't it?

Cheap date. Very cheap. It may have cost him absolutely nothing.

You may have gone to the grocery store and took the groceries over to his house, and never asked that man for a dime. And you, Player, knew she couldn't afford to feed you steaks and lobster. She already has two kids and no outside support. But she never asked, and you never offered.

She thought you had class, but obviously you don't. You don't even have common decency. Because you're a physical spirit spouse; you're a taker, a user--, you're a player.

    She bought the groceries, brought the groceries to his house, cleaned up afterward, and then entertained him to the max. It's all TOO MUCH, and it is not of God. She's not your wife and you're not her husband; you don't deserve any of that.

    But now he's gone, and she still may be wondering what's wrong with her. She may be making herself over to look the way your demons want her to dress, but that wasn't her nature at that time, was it? Has she changed, because you told her that she wasn't hot enough –so she's changed her hair, nails, makeup, attitude, and wearing tight, tight clothes. She's not even realizing she will now start to attract more people with the same **demons** that you have.

    Women, don't act like you don't know what I'm talking about --, you know the things that men have tried to convince you to wear.

No matter how cute she still is, no matter how she dresses, she's only now attracting married guys and old guys because her GLORY is gone. Her glory has been stolen by a player, or more than one player over the years.

Players gonna play.

Or if she really goes into the flesh, she's seeking revenge. She may be planning a Louisville slugger moment for your car or other property.

She may be getting into a beef with your new girlfriend. Or, she may have just given in to grief, despair, and depression, she may have quit school, quit church, and moved back in with her folks.

The player is gone, and he doesn't care. Anything she does PROVES that she is crazy, and he **HAD** to leave her. Ladies, this is not a winning situation, no matter how you look at it.

That man, if he is doing what every other carnal man is doing, what every player and what every OG is doing trying to feed *lust* – it is impossible, lust will NEVER be satisfied. NEVER. You are not doing anything.

Lust is one of the idols of the land, it has never, and will never have enough of anything. There you are working like the devil to satisfy something that cannot be satisfied. Lust in any relationship or marriage will be the cause of the failure of that marriage.

If you are not doing what God said do with the wife of your youth, then you are working for the devil. Yeah, not just single women get traumatized, a married woman can experience relationship trauma in any number of ways.

IT'S ALL TOO MUCH.

Sinvitations

Most places have their own reputation. Sin City is not just one place; there are many sin cities. Speaking to a young lady the other day, she revealed that her desire at this point in her life is to go to a number of travel destinations. They are all party cities, sin cities. She's not even of drinking age yet, but look at what is in her blood. Her blood is drawing her to those places. Said another way, what is in her blood is calling her to those places. She's getting **SINVITATIONS** and she's not even a legal adult yet.

Men, if you're doing what every other OG, rolling stone, and player--, what every other carnal, flesh-driven man is doing, trying to feed the *lust* that is in you -- you ain't doing nothing.

LUST IS ONE OF THE IDOLS OF THE LAND. If it is calling you, obviously that's what is in you. Since the ways of a man are clean in his own eyes, you don't see anything wrong with what you want to do, or what you do. It's why we need a real pastor, turn on Holy Spirit Notifications, and also one another ministry, so people can tell you the truth in Love.

Sin is by invitation. *Sinvitations* come at humans all day and all night 24/7. A human doesn't get the idea to sin on his or her own, it is an escorted enticement. When it comes to dating, sex, fornication and adultery, the sin will be against the person's body.

The idols of the land, territorial idols, ancestral, family idols, idols of your father's house are sending *sinvitations* to you daily, nightly, even while you are asleep.

Lust will never have enough. Not enough **anything**. Never. You cannot appease it, and there you are working like the devil to satisfy something that cannot be satisfied.

If you are not doing what God said to do toward the wife of your youth, you are working for the devil. (Proverbs 5:18-19)

If you don't have love and can't be in a loving relationship, then you have nothing, you are nothing. (1 Corinthians 13)

I've warned the ladies and also now the men, if you are in a relationship with someone who doesn't know what love is, can't love, and doesn't love you – they never say they love you, they never *do*, I love you, RUN!

If you have to constantly ask someone with whom you are in a "relationship" if they love you. Get out of that relationship.

RUN!

Polygamous People

Polygamous men create traumas and problems for everyone they encounter and try to get in relationship with.

Poly-, any kind of people -- you are creating problems that when you get older you will see the devastation of what you are choosing to do today. You may end up being one of those people calling somebody for prayer and deliverance. When you enter into crisis, whip out that God card--, no, get saved and establish relationship with God. Walk upright before God and He will keep your life from falling into disaster. But if you need deliverance, get it.

These results don't need to be tested or retested. Just listen to what people who have been *through* have to say about dating and relationships. Hear what older folks have to say. Most younger people, myself included, used to think that older folks just said all this kind of stuff because they were old, and have had their fun and just don't want young people to have any fun.

NO, OLDER FOLKS ARE TELLING YOU THIS STUFF BECAUSE THEY JUST NOW FIGURED IT OUT—after all of these years, all of these decades. They WISH THEY HADN'T DONE a whole lot of stuff they did WHEN THEY WERE YOUNG. Because of where they are now, because of what they are experiencing now, it is diminishing their life – their lives are not as they thought it would be.

Most, if not all, wish they had listened to their parents and elders when they were young.

It can take a long time to see the results of being rebellious and sinful – the devil wouldn't want you to find out too quickly, else, you'd stop in your 20's instead of continuing to do the same stuff into your 40's or beyond. Yeah, there are OG's still out here older than 40, past 50--, some older than that. They are on assignment and may not realize it.

How can I say that?

When any person looks at their own body of work, should they not judge it?

When a confirmed bachelor, or cheating, so-called married man looks at the relationships that he's entered in throughout his lifetime, what must he see, if he honestly assesses them? He can't look at them from his point of view only, but from the perspective of each of the ladies. How did he find them, compared to how he left them? If all of them are worse in any way, emotionally, socially, physically, financially, or especially spiritually, he is a trauma agent for the devil.

So here comes some silver fox, or some young cute guy; it's a trap. Even though some call women traps, it is not always the lady, but it can be. Delilah knows. The devil lays back and watches you walk into the snare he's set for you, pretending *he* didn't set the snare, and pretending he doesn't see you right there in it. By the time you get comfortable thinking nothing is going to get you, you're fully in his trap, and a lot of years may have gone by.

That young guy, that bad boy, even that silver fox, or zaddy--, yeah, he's cute, and he knows it. How many bad boys are ugly? He's supposed to be good looking, that is by design. How is the devil going to trap you with an ugly person, or a person who is not attractive to you?

And, yes, he's cool and has swag – all that is pride, false pride and it is all demonic. It is charged to attract the opposite gender--.

That trauma agent's assignment is to enter into as many relationships or situationships as possible, that is, be polygamous.

This is totally not of God.

Adam & Eve were in the Garden – when God asked Adam, **What have you done?** Adam said, God, that woman you gave me.

Please note here that Adam Didn't Say**, GOD – YOU ONLY GAVE ME ONE WOMAN, and that's why I had to sin**. Adam never said, God you only gave me one woman and that is why I had to sin. Because Adam wasn't created with the *spirit of lust* and didn't have the *spirit of lust* --, at that time.

This bunch of wives thing, polygamy – that's a man-made construct under the guise of needing heirs. GOD, in His Wisdom, said be the husband of **one wife.**

A bishop then must be blameless, the husband of one wife, vigilant, sober, of good behaviour, given to hospitality, apt to teach; (1 Timothy 3:2)

Being a bishop doesn't mean the bishop necessarily of a church, but it does. Husbands, you are the bishop of your homes, you are the bishop of the souls in your home; you are responsible for them.

Let the deacons be the husbands of one wife, ruling their children and their own houses well, (1 Timothy 3:12)

If any be blameless, the husband of one wife, having faithful children not accused of riot or unruly, (Titus 1:6)

You need to be raising your kids, not out in the streets raising Cain.

One wife means one wife at a time, that does not mean that the person only married one time. God does allow divorce, I go into this in depth in my book, **Second Marriage, Third Marriage, Any Marriage.**

The devil's trauma agent is a bad boy and has bad *spirits*. He will remain a bad boy unless he gets saved *and* delivered, you can't save him, only Jesus. Until then all those *spirits* can transfer to you, as you take on his *nature by taking on the nature of his idols*. And that is how you learn how to be like him. That is how you learn how to give it back to him just as he dishes it out to you. The spiritual transference is complete.

How are you going to get rid of them? It's going to take some work. Some only come out by prayer and fasting.

You may be wondering, what if I get saved, won't those *spirits* just go away?

Spirits can be suppressed, they can hide… they can wait for the opportunity to act out again at the worst time. Especially if you entertain them at all. Entertaining them, listening to them, doing what they want you to do is worship. You worship a demon, that's like feeding a stray cat. It is not going anywhere.

This guy who is out there without spiritual covering, and with poor guidance is about the most dangerous person you could meet and get with because he has no Godly spiritual protection. He might have idol *gods* that he believes in, but if Jehovah is not his God, he has no spiritual protection and no proper spiritual guidance, therefore ANYTHING could be in his life, and in him. He could track all of that dirt into your house and your life. You should RUN.

Lust is definitely his little g *god*, among others. *Lust* can't protect him from anything; it only gets him into **more trouble.**

Anything could be after him and hanging on to him. Anything could be looking for him to attack and attach to him, and you do not want to be collateral damage – just by being in the vicinity or associated with him.

(Hear me, I've done all this stuff, I'm not just talking--, I know what I'm talking about.)

Anyone could be after him--, and he is unprotected. He's an outlaw to God, and witchcraft arrows can hit him and whomever is associated with him.

Additionally, <u>you</u> don't want to have to be <u>*his*</u> spiritual protection, when as a man, he should be yours.

If you are following Jehovah and he's worshipping idol *gods*, he will want to know sooner than later, why aren't you worshipping the same idol *gods* as him? Why don't you follow the celebrities, the sports stars, the musical artists that he adores? Why don't you want to go to a concert every week and worship at the throne of a rap or other musician? Why don't you ever want to have any fun? *It's just a little weed. Come on, have some drinks with me.*

Why don't we do something to spice up the bedroom? He is trying to introduce you to more idol *gods*. Watch this show with me. These idol *gods*, are either already in good with him, or introducing themselves to him. They are idols of the land, and they are *sinviting* him. As he meets them, and enjoys them (at first) he in turn is d'evangelizing you, and *sinviting* you to go away from God and worship them, too.

The idols of the land are calling to mankind, 24/7, sinviting us day and night.

Over time, he (and his demons) will become angry that he is not leading, even if that leading is leading you, him, or both of you straight to hell.

You want to do all the praying in the relationship? All the Bible reading, and have no one to discuss anything spiritual with? He won't know what you're talking about. Spiritual things are foolishness to the carnal man. I don't care how cute he is, how much fun he is, this will lead to dating trauma, or relationship trauma.

Unless this is a physically abusive man, all your injuries will be soft tissue injuries. Soft tissue trauma is still trauma. Your heart is a soft tissue. Your feelings, your emotions are soft tissue. No one can see them, but you feel the hurt, nonetheless. You may feel the hurt all the more.

This is such an uneven yoke. A bad yoke is not a joke. I don't care how cute, or successful or fun he is. Players deliver trauma, and that's just more work for you to try to get out of those kinds of spiritual traps.

He's My Covering, *Right*?

I want to put this delicately, woman of God, we are told to marry, and it is in us to seek our Kingdom spouse. I believe all that is normal. But we can't seek that Kingdom mate at all costs, with reckless abandon. Just because you get a husband, get the man, or close the deal doesn't negate or absolve you of all the sin that you incurred or chose to do in the process of **getting** the husband.

That you close the deal doesn't liberate you from the iniquity of whatever sins you participated in, or allowed into your life because you wanted to please the man.

While you are single, your primary goal should be to please God. The Word says that the married woman seeks to please her husband, that married woman still has to pick and choose what she will do to please him. If he asks her to sin, will she--, she can't say, *God that man you gave me caused me to sin,* any more than Adam could say that about Eve.

He asks you to rob a bank, steal from the mall, do drugs, have a menage a trois, lie for him as an alibi or on important documents—and you do any or all of this. All of the consequences of having done any of those things is still going to come back on you. Just because he is a man, and note, only a man, he cannot stop spiritual things that are spiritual law from happening to you.

So, there is no reason to put this man before God and do things that you know better than to do, as if God is only going to ask that man what in the world was ***he*** thinking, and never come to you.

He's your covering? Yes, if you are married. By covering it doesn't mean he takes the rap for you, he doesn't take the fall instead of you – that's what Jesus did for us. By covering, this man should PROTECT you from doing things that would allow the devil in to steal, kill, and destroy you or any part of your life.

If this man is not spiritually connected to God, he's not covered himself. How can he possibly cover you if he's not covered?

License to Thrill

Yeah, but he's got that golden touch.

Of course, he does. He's not just very well practiced, he is also demonically charged. Enhanced... for your pleasure, enjoyment... and your addiction... this is part of the devil's plan.

He will tell you that you're the best he's ever had, and you will believe it. He's supposed to say that; it's in his script, and it works. You believe what he said and now you get comfortable thinking you two are in a real relationship, thinking he will always be with you, stay with you, come back to you. So you open up your whole soul, your whole life and you give him the best that you've got. EVEN THOUGH you're not his wife and he's not your husband, he shouldn't be getting any of that from you.

This bad boy has demonic assist to thrill you, to capture you. You may not notice that, but he is SO different from what you've had before, and for some reason he knows EXACTLY what buttons to push on you. Why is that? Have you ever considered that?

It is by design, he has demonic charge, demonic assist. *Familiar spirits* that have been studying you all your life are communicating with his *familiar spirits*. This guy might not even know why he is doing this that or the other with you or to you, he is just doing it. He thinks he's lucky. You think he's *all that*. It's demonic. You don't think God blessed an unsaved player to be the best you ever had so this player could take advantage of you, do you?

That doesn't mean that marital relations can't be exciting and meaningful, but I'm talking about these rando player types who blow into your life, blow your mind, traumatize, and upset your life, and then they are gone. Mr. Magic, in the natural.

Mr. Magic in the dream—that's spirit spouse. You do not need to have a dream of having relations with your own husband. That is a masquerade. You've got to pray and stay prayed up.

Bed Defilement

> Marriage *is* honorable among all, and the bed undefiled; but fornicators and adulterers God will judge. Hebrews 13:4

A man tried to talk his wife into all sorts of stuff in the bedroom. He used Scripture to do it. His oft used quote was the above verse, The marriage bed is undefiled. By using it, he meant that *anything goes* in the bedroom of a married couple.

That is not true. A kingdom couple in a kingdom marriage cannot do ungodly things in their bedroom and believe it is sanctified because they are married. Just by doing any ungodly act, they invite demons, such as *spirit spouses*, and all kinds of evil into the act.

If pregnancy results from that union with the devil in it, they just let the devil have access to their child.

The marriage bed should not be defiled, but it can be with defiled acts, thoughts, and et cetera. The correct understanding of that verse is that the marriage bed is **to be** undefiled. It is foolhardy to think that God will sanctify absolutely anything that a married couple does. If that were the case everyone could just get married and sin to their flesh's content. But that is not possible.

Sin is sin, no matter where and no matter who with; it is still sin.

If the devil has figured out a way to get demons into a person by sex, wouldn't he perfect his M.O. regarding sex and humans?

The marriage bed is undefiled...God said stay away from: fornication and adultery. Pornography is adultery. He who has looked on a woman to lust after her has already sinned.

But I say unto you, That whosoever looketh on a woman to lust after her hath committed adultery with her already in his heart, (Matthew 5:28)

Are you planning to or bringing your spouse into the **same** bed where you've had multiple conquests? Where you have invited *spirit spouse* by watching pornography and other racy shows? Where you have masturbated and conjured up the Lord knows what? Have you made your bed into an altar by having had so many relations with so many people who themselves have their own sets of *spirits* attached? How many demons have transferred back and forth in that room? How many remain? If this bed is an altar, who is the sacrifice? You? Your new spouse?

Prayer treatment is needed for you, your marriage, your union, your house, your bedroom, your bed, your mattress--, get new sheets and covers. Burn the old stuff. The foundation that you may be starting your marriage out on may be faulty and it will lead to fights, arguments, disagreements, and possibly separation and divorce. The bed is defiled. Are either of you defiled? The mattress is defiled. The sheets, and pillows are defiled.

As a matter of course, consecrate ay new items you buy for your marital bedroom. Righteous seed cannot come out of defiled people, or even out of one defiled person. One sinner destroys much good.

As you start your Kingdom marriage, bless your house, of course, but consecrate your marriage bed, actually all your furnishings, as well.

Married to the Mob

A fellow who is hopping from one woman to the next may not be able to help himself: it's a spirit—at least one, *lust*). If it is not the Spirit of God, you really don't want it.

The idolater is married to some of these idols, if he's got his own *spirit spouse* that spirit spouse doesn't want him to get a wife. Her job is to tell him that he can't get married in the natural and be tied down – with the same woman all his life!??? That's *spirit spouse* talk. Do you realize how much money is wasted on jumping around from house to house and relationship to relationship? That is one of the ways *spirit spouse* steals money from people. Those who, yes, settle down and become stable and build with the spouse of their youth are far better off in many ways, especially financially by middle age and in their golden years.

Plus, this rolling stone, player type is already married to *spirit spouse*—in the spirit. This fellow, and anyone who believes the rhetoric of a *spirit spouse* is doomed for bad relationships and to either be traumatized in them or be the one traumatizing the other.

When I say, believe the rhetoric of *spirit spouse* I mean all of us must consider and judge the source of the thoughts that come to us. Mankind is fed thoughts all day long. If Christ is on the Throne of your heart and there is no other *spirit* in you other than the Holy Spirit, the thoughts and inclinations that come to you will all be of God.

Jesus is the only person who can say that He only has one Spirit, and that is the Holy Spirit, because fallen man, and that's all of us, have voices coming to us from many sources.

Our soul has a voice and speaks. Its why you have to command your soul to do things, including to bless the Lord. Else, your soul may obey the *spirits* that inhabit it. There could be a mob of *spirits* in anyone at any time, all demanding attention and obedience to what they want you to do.

Our flesh is forever making demands and is talking to us. Food, beverage and sex cravings are most often influences of the flesh.

Any *spirit* that is near or in us is also speaking. A *spirit spouse* will tell you all day long what is wrong with even your own legal spouse, why they are not right for you, or not good enough for you, or that you deserve better and can do better. Your spouse is not hot enough, fun enough, or doing enough in the relationship. When you believe the whispers and demonic dreams sponsored by *spirit spouse* (because they can do that, too), you will begin to **hate** your real marriage partner, or even the person you are dating and planning to marry.

As long as he is going from woman to woman, person to person and nothing is serious, *spirit spouse* is happy and they will seem to coexist, even though *spirit spouse* is running things, but the human thinks *they got this*. Well, they will seem to get along, until they don't.

But if he gets serious about somebody – it's going to be bad.

Ladies, let's say you do close the deal and get married to a guy with a *spirit spouse*. There are a mob of other *spirits* in anyone who has even one evil *spirit*; they travel in packs. Also, a person can have more than one *spirit spouse*; there can be many. Any idol *god* that "marries" a person, whether it elicits sexual arousal, sexual feelings, or actual sex in the dream, and in some cases, sex in the natural, is considered a *spirit spouse*.

For our example, let's say this guy has no spiritual knowledge, no knowledge of *spirit spouse,* what it is or that it exists, but if he did, -- he's not saved, he has no salvation and no inclination to pray about it. You've got to do all the praying; however, you cannot make him do anything against his own will. If you did, that would be witchcraft. So as long as your spouse is content, okay with, or not rejecting *spirit spouse*, he will keep *spirit spouse*, no matter how much **you** pray.

Let's say you, even in your salvation and in your prayed up life, you have a *spirit spouse* too, whether you know about it or not. You may know about it--, you may be getting sex in the dream, sleep paralysis, or other signs of *spirit spouse*. You may be trying to rid yourself of it.

You may not even know you have one–, perhaps your dreams are being wiped. Maybe it came down your ancestral line, or you've got sins of your youth that you haven't figured out how to deal with yet. **CAN YOU IMAGINE THE FIGHTS IN YOUR HOUSE?** Each *spirit spouse* wants to get rid of the natural spouse – either break up the relationship, or get rid of the other person PERMANENTLY. *Spirit spouse* is jealous, violent, ruthless, desperate to stay in the "house" (you) where it believes it has married you, and does not care about the permanent loss of another human being.

Victims of players, OG's and such, cut your losses. Get out of those situationships, get out of those so-called relationships. Repent to God; break soul ties, move on with your life. **Don't let player drama and dating trauma stagnate your life or steal your future.**

To want to get married, and have children is normal, anything else, is not of God. Rolling stones may be exciting for a season, while you're in sin, yourself, you won't see anything wrong with them. If you are a novice to salvation, you may keep a player around because you think you can save them, change them, rehabilitate them. You can't-- not against their own free will and not without them accepting Jesus Christ and submitting to change. Cut your losses; keep it moving. Spending too much time in bad relationships and with bad boys (or girls) is how time is wasted and lost. It is how glory, purpose and destinies are stolen. Don't do it.

If you try to trick or force a demonized person to marry you, for any reason—so they can change or so the other girlfriend doesn't, it's going to be like cornering a wild animal, not because of the person, not because of the human being, but because of the *spirits* that are in that person. Demons riot, they flare up, they react, and they fight dirty. They are jealous and they are strong, get rid of *spirit spouse*, and other idol *gods* that may have taken up residence in your life (or body), the right way. Pray. Fast & Pray. Seek deliverance if they resist and don't leave.

Don't force marriage with someone with a *spirit spouse*. Further, get rid of your own so you will be desirable to a Kingdom spouse, yourself.

Think about that because the devil loves trauma, even soft tissue damage --- and if he can traumatize people, he can get into their lives, mess them up, steal from them, or kill them if he gets the opportunity.

So, your job is to recognize a player, whether he (or she) knows that they are a player or not. Pray for them, if God agrees, but keep it moving, and live your own successful life.

Make It Stop!

There is no age limit on this crazy player behavior. Players age into silver foxes and OG's. Once a player, until delivered, always a player. The only other thing, sexually speaking, that stops a player besides salvation and deliverance is pretty much when stuff just doesn't work anymore.

Now king David was old *and* stricken in years; and they covered him with clothes, but he gat no heat.

Wherefore his servants said unto him, Let there be sought for my lord the king a young virgin: and let her stand before the king, and let her cherish him, and let her lie in thy bosom, that my lord the king may get heat.

So they sought for a fair damsel throughout all the coasts of Israel, and found Abishag a Shunammite, and brought her to the king.

And the damsel *was* very fair, and cherished the king, and ministered to him: but the king knew her not, (1King???

David didn't *get with* this young woman because he couldn't, his stuff had stopped working. But you see how his advisors had the same idea as players today – go get another woman. Go get a more beautiful woman. Go get a young or younger woman.

Women, do you see how an ungodly, non-committed man will see your life as disposable? He may see it as something to be used and then tossed away? Therefore, you must put value on yourself and your own life, and not even let it be disposable for a season. Do not waste your own time, and certainly let no one else waste it. Do not let your beauty, youth, or virtues be used or wasted. Do not deceive yourself in to thinking I know he's not right today, but I'll be so good to him that he will change. Oh, that's perfect for a user, you are the exact right type that he will use and walk away from. He may have 5 or 10 women working hard to please him in to being a decent man, staying with them, or marrying them. You didn't invent this; sorry.

You have value; ask God to show you your value and God's plans and purposes for your life. Do not let a demonized dude tell you. Do not let anyone other than God define your value, purpose, and life.

But when a man's *stuff* stops working, this is often an act of *spirit spouse* as well. She can make a man unresponsive to humans. I don't know if you know how many witchcraft attacks against men include this desire.

A male *spirit spouse* will do the same to a female victim. This is why you see many people desire to be "alone" rather than with their own spouse. *Spirit spouse* is the cause of pain during relations for women, and can transfer dreadful mystery diseases to both male and female victims.

Spirit spouse is disgusting.

Sometimes the only thing that stops a player is when the player's stuff stops working. If spirit spouse has been given any control or permission in that area of a person's life, *spirit spouse* can turn human libido on or OFF at will. This is no laughing matter. The devil does not want righteous seed to come to the Earth, so turning off desire and relations between a husband and a wife is a master stroke of warfare.

Do you see now why you must shun sin, resist the devil, and stay prayed up? Even that first swipe right signed you up for all kinds of unwritten *future* evil.

There will always be old players out in the world. There will always be the oldest guy at the club, especially now that they have invented little blue pills that help a man "get heat" well into his golden years.

And what is that man looking for? Abishag, some young girl either poor enough or dumb enough to fall for his lines. As soon as a man thinks that he's not "getting heat" he decides he needs a new model, as if a wife is a car, or a furnace to make him look good, or keep him warm.

Discern every *spirit*. Even the "mature" single has decided it's time to come in from the cold, coming in off the streets, and FINALLY hanging up his player hat, that does not mean he knows how or is ready for a **relationship**. Check with GOD first. Pray, find out the motives of any person.

Sex is still the #1 way the devil can move *spirits* in and out of folks. Players are out in the world in abundance, looking to get in wherever they can fit in. Don't be their victim.

Please pray that you haven't opened your very SOUL, the seat of your being up to a demon or a bunch of demonic *spirits* under the guise of DATING.

Dating can be traumatic; but, it doesn't have to be. God can fix it so you meet and date the right person, and never be traumatized in the process.

Lord, be with us all and help us heal from every trauma and still go on to fulfill Your will for our lives, in the Name of Jesus.

Amen.

The following prayer is excerpted from the book, **The Devil Loves Trauma**, as these two books are very much connected.

Let's Get Healed of Traumas

Father in the Name of Jesus Christ, and by the power of His Cross and His Blood, we bind up the power of any evil *spirit*, and command them not to block our prayers.

We bind the power of Earth, air, water, fire, the netherworld, and the satanic forces of nature. We break any curses, hexes, or spells sent against us and declare them null and void.

We break the assignments of any *spirits* sent against us and send them to Jesus to deal with them, as He will.

We ask You to bless our enemies by sending your Holy Spirit to lead those who will repent, to repentance and conversion.

Lord, I bind all interaction and communication of *evil* human spirits as it pertains to me.

I ask for the protection of the shed Blood of Jesus Christ as I pray this prayer.

Thank You, Lord, for divine protection. Send Your warrior angels to give me the win in this battle.

In the Name of Jesus Christ, I command you devil, not to interfere with this prayer. I cut you off by the Sword of the Spirit from the stirring up of grief, fear, fear of any kind, emotional, or any other kind of trauma induced problems, and I command quiet, in the Name of Jesus.

Lord, in the Name of Jesus, I forgive everyone who has offended, hurt, harmed, embarrassed, or traumatized me in any way.

Lord, go back to the moment in time of this trauma, to that broken relationship, that broken heart, the disappointment, the loss, the sadness that continues to influence me, Lord. Jesus, take the sting, the bite, the hurt, the pain, the trauma, the loss out of that event so it no longer harms me.

Lord, transform that day, that hour, that moment, that event in my mind and let me see that if You allowed it, You used it to bless me or teach me and enlarge me. Lord, let me see You there. In that moment, in that time, ministering to me right at that time.

I know You were there. You would never leave me or forsake me.

Lord, forgive me for my part in allowing that evil to come upon my life.

And I know that what the devil meant for evil, what he meant for my harm, that You can turn it for my good.

Spirit of Trauma, exit my life now, exit my life forever. The angels of God escort you out now and take you to the place assigned to you. It is not with me. Not any longer.

Spirit of grief, Exit my life now. Exit my life forever. The angels of God escort you out now and take you to the place assigned for you. It is not with me. Not any longer.

Spirit of loss, sadness, disappointment, sympathy, exit my life now. Exit my life forever. The angels of God escort you out now and take you to the place assigned for you. It is not with me. Not any longer.

Spirit of fear, exit my life now. Exit my life forever. The angels of God escort you out now and take you to the place assigned for you. It is not with me. Not any longer.

Spirits of incest, rape, abuse, domestic violence, domestic terrorism, exit my life now. Exit my life forever. The angels of God escort you out now and take you to the place assigned for you. It is not with me. Not any longer.

Wounds infected by evil, you are now healed, in the Name of Jesus.

Holy Ghost, fill me. Fill me with Your Spirit, Your Power, Your Grace, Your Peace, Your comfort, to overflowing, that I pour it out to others, in the Name of Jesus.

Lord, do a new thing in me today. Break me out of old patterns and flesh reactions. Lord, give me the Mind of Christ and the ability to respond to life's stresses in a Godly way, in an unpredictable way, so the devil can not guess what I will do next, in the Name of Jesus.

Any attacks because of these prayers, I command those attacks to backfire, in the Name of Jesus.

I seal these declarations across every realm, age, dimension, and timeline, past, present, and future, to infinity, in the matchless Name of Jesus Christ.

Amen.

There are more prayers on Warfare Prayer Channel, as well as messages on DrMiles Channel, both on YouTube. Some other topics and titles of videos are:

Prayer Resources

Prayers against dream defilement: https://www.youtube.com/watch?v=b7s5UJ74REo&t=2207s

Prayers against sex in the dream:

https://www.youtube.com/watch?v=pOl9-JBdj_E&t=6228s

Prayers to divorce spirit spouse:

https://www.youtube.com/watch?v=8TZkt4RatWQ&t=137s

Prayers against the evil marine kingdom:

https://www.youtube.com/watch?v=hHnpEsq3mZg&t=1139s

Prayers for a kingdom marriage:

https://www.youtube.com/watch?v=ClyxEnGZTCM

Prayers against barrenness:

https://www.youtube.com/watch?v=BMSMBMCp0qQ

Prayers for a fruitful womb:

https://www.youtube.com/watch?v=IZlr_s3jkog&t=830s

Dear Reader:

Thank you for acquiring and reading this book. I pray the Lord for your peace and deliverance from every evil plan of the enemy. I pray that you will use Wisdom and discernment always so that no weapon that is formed against you will ever prosper.

Shalom,

Dr. Marlene Miles

Other books by this author

AK: Adventures of the Agape Kid

AMONG SOME THIEVES

As My Soul Prospers

Behave

Blindsided: Has the Old Man Bewitched You?

Churchzilla (The Wanna-Be Bride of Christ)

The Coco-So-So Correct Show

Demons Hate Questions

Devil Loves Trauma, *The*

Do Not Orphan Your Seed

Do Not Work for Money

Don't Refuse Me Lord

EVIL TOUCH

The FAT Demons

got Money?

Let Me Have a Dollar's Worth

Living for the NOW of God

Lord, Help My Debt

Lose My Location

Made Perfect In Love

The Man Safari *(Really, I'm Just Looking)*

Marriage Ed., *Rules of Engagement & Marriage*

The Motherboard: *Key to Soul Prosperity*

Name Your Seed

Plantation Souls

The Poor Attitudes of Money

Power Money: Nine Times the Tithe

Seasons of Grief

Seasons of War

SOULS in Captivity

Soul Prosperity: Your Health & Your Wealth

The *spirit* of Poverty

The Throne of Grace, *Courtroom Prayers*

Warfare Prayer Against Poverty

When the Devourer is Rebuked

The Wilderness Romance 3-book series, *The Social Wilderness, The Sexual Wilderness & The Spiritual Wilderness.*

Cover art for Players Gonna Play:
Illustration 18814642 © Mijo69 | Dreamstime.com

ID1380757 © Remster |Dreamstime.com

www.ingramcontent.com/pod-product-compliance
Lightning Source LLC
Chambersburg PA
CBHW070855050426
42453CB00012B/2208